THE

"Make Me Good with Money!"

BOOK

Easy steps for taking you to where the Money resides!

KArima Mckenzie-Thomas

THE "Make Me Good with Money" BOOK

KArima McKenzie-Thomas

Copyright © 2019-2021 KArima McKenzie-Thomas. All rights reserved.

THE "Make Me Good with Money" BOOK

KArima McKenzie-Thomas

THE "Make Me Good with Money" BOOK

This book was inspired by my mother the banker who didn't know what she didn't know, but tried her very best.

Preface

With the huge number of Money books already in existence, one of the first questions you would rightly ask is "Why?" Why would someone write yet another book on Money, and what makes this one so important for you to read?

Well, I'm the girl who made well over a third of a million dollars in 18 months at the age of 30 offering Social Media and Marketing services to corporate clients; and by 31, had nothing to show for it financially. If you'd met me at 31, you'd

NEVER know my lifestyle had been TOTALLY different just a few short months before.

I'm also the girl who has been homeless at various times, both by myself AND with my young child and even slept with my child on a friend's couch for a week, because I didn't have Money to pay my few hundred-dollar electricity bill. Clearly the friend didn't have it to lend either. They really DO say that your finances reflect the finances of the 5 people you spend the most time with. Go figure.

Finally, after years of research, learning and trial and error around Money, I'm the girl who overcame all that to get to the point where I began growing my Money monthly at a 15% interest rate during a recession - at a time when financial institutions nationwide were boasting about giving their clients 3% and 5% returns on their money. Realizing consistent success after a year and a half, I took on investors and began giving them an 8% return on their Money. I then went on to self-fund a restaurant operation which I closed after a year because the rate of return vs work just wasn't enough for me.

This turn around in my finances was not just by accident or luck, so let me take a moment to acknowledge the privileges that I know helped me to get there:

Apart from my awesome ability (inherited from my parents) to consume and process large amounts of information and use it to improve my life, because of who my parents are and who they made me, I am fortunate to have some millionaires and successful businesspeople in my network that I was able to observe and learn from as they conducted their day-to-day affairs. I also attended a high school where I interacted daily with many East Indians and their parents, giving me the opportunity to observe how the East Indian community lives and how they deal with Money, and to compare and contrast with what I've seen others do.

All this first-hand experience, observation and knowledge are what you will find in the following pages. The principles I have learned and continue to apply in my own life, the knowledge that has opened my eyes to the harmful myths so many of us have been conditioned to see as true, and the information I have used to positively grow my net worth - I have all broken down within the covers of this book.

My most sincere hope is that this book opens the financial eyes and possibilities of people across the world, empowering them to totally control their financial destinies, and to even create wealth.

Happy reading.

K. Mck-T

KArima McKenzie-Thomas

THE "Make Me Good with Money" BOOK

Acknowledgements

I'd like to first of all thank my parents who because of their example, pushed me to figure out what Money is and how to leverage it, so that I could have a financially comfortable life and do better than they did.

My deepest appreciation to my crew of proofreaders. You're rock stars and your feedback was invaluable; thank you.

Many thanks to my ladies who so generously shared the Money wisdom that has helped them throughout life. Your generosity will help many.

Thank you, thank you, thank you to Amanda, Marcella, Rhoda, Valisha and everyone else who allowed me to share my newfound Money wisdom with them over the years and who gave such enthusiastic feedback as the wisdom began turning their finances around in ways small and not so small. I heart all of you.

And...thank YOU dear reader. This book is yours. It was specifically envisioned, written and published for you – to help you and to positively impact your life now and in the future, by improving your financial life.

THE "Make Me Good with Money" BOOK

Table of Contents

Chapter 1

> **"What is this damn thing anyway?"**

Chapter 2

> **"I need help. Where do I begin?"**

Chapter 3

> **"Ground-Zero"**

Chapter 4

> **"Wait, you're trying to say that there are people who have no debt? HOW??"**

Chapter 5

> **"What do the wealthy do with Money?"**

Chapter 6

> **"More About Debt"**

Chapter 7

> **"Make a Decision."**

Chapter 8

> **"Containers"**

Chapter 9

> **"But I have lots of debt – what do I do?"**

Chapter 10

> **"Moving Forward."**

Chapter 11

> **"An Alternative Financial Map"**

Chapter 12

> **"Keep Learning."**

Money Wisdom

Glossary

KArima McKenzie-Thomas

THE "Make Me Good with Money" BOOK

KArima McKenzie-Thomas

Introduction

"... but Money answereth all things".

Excerpted from Ecclesiastes 10 vs 19.

Money.

Is there a topic - apart from Love - that causes more drama, fear, jealousy, anger, confusion, guilt and judgement? I doubt it.

In the Caribbean where I'm from, it's not strange to hear reports of choppings related to Money and land in the news, or to overhear angry outbursts about politicians misusing Money as you walk around town. Also, how many of us as children were told some version of *"Chile, you feel Money does grow on trees or what?"*

From childhood, most of us have had a love/hate relationship with the resource, the energy called Money that we can't live without, but don't know how to properly live with.

This book seeks to help with that issue, offering you -

- A deeper understanding of what Money is, and

- Information on how best to use Money for building a sound financial foundation and to guarantee you a secure, comfortable future.

It walks you through a better appreciation of what Money is and gives specific information on how to use it for building a sound financial foundation and guaranteeing yourself a secure, comfortable future.

I also share personal advice from some women in my network whom I admire and who have successfully figured out how to use Money to ensure their best futures, even while affording comfortable and enjoyable lives in the present.

Be warned - this book is not a coffee table quick read! You are meant to workshop your way through the chapters, examining yourself, your habits and your beliefs, figuring out where you've been going wrong, and making the necessary adjustments to become better and do better.

Mistakes are inevitable but crashing and burning is not. If you make a mistake or find yourself backtracking into a bad habit or poor thinking, just stop it right then and there, dust yourself off and do better tomorrow. That's it. No wallowing in your mistake, no drama, no quitting. This is your best future we're working on here, and we have no time for flakiness!

Get your notebook, organize your book club and/or accountability partner(s) and let's go!!!

See you on the other side.

KAramel

THE "Make Me Good with Money" BOOK

Chapter 1

"What is this damn thing anyway?"

Money.

Some say it is a tool – there to be leveraged for living your best life. Others say it's energy – flowing to and through you, attracted or repelled by your habits, thoughts, beliefs and feelings. There are those who feel amassing lots of it is their birth right, and others who are mortally afraid of having too much.

From observation and experience I've actually found that the energy Money carries is identical to that of water. Yes, water. Hell, we even say that Money flows!

Let's go further into that concept and see if you don't agree with me by the end.

What are the properties of water?

- Water is a resource, naturally occurring, abundant and renewable.

- Water takes various forms – e.g. solid, liquid, gas – and if you think about it, water is always there, surrounding us, in one form or another.

- Water must be respected and used with reverence, as all the indigenous peoples of the world knew. Many of them even worshipped it.

- Water should NEVER be prevented from flowing, because stagnant water brings decay, death and disease.

- In order to have all the water we need we must collect it in the necessary amounts and sizes of containers. Therefore, we must first be abundantly clear on exactly *what* we require water for.

- To collect it, we must also have a plan – is it rain, river or pumped water that we will be collecting, or perhaps from a combination of sources? Who will do the collecting? Do we require any special equipment or knowledge? Are our containers the correct size? How are we getting the water from our containers to wherever we need it – e.g. kitchen, bathroom, plant beds, etc.?

- We must ALWAYS be careful not to misuse and waste water because as we have seen, this has negative impacts both on us in the future and on generations to come.

If you took a look at the list above and swapped out the word **Money** wherever you see the word water, does the concept suddenly make complete sense? Try it!

$$$

Activity 1.1

Write down each Money statement from above and read it out loud. Observe what emotions or thoughts come up for you:

- Any disbelief?

- Negative responses?

- Confusion?

- Agreement?

- What else?

Take note of all those thoughts and feelings because we will be examining them later on.

$$$

Right, so now that I've shaken up your concept of Money a little bit, let's go even further.

Apart from all the things above, Money is a mirror. The way you treat and use Money shows the world very clearly who you think you are and what you think you deserve.

Let me explain - those who spend Money frivolously are saying to the world and to the Universe that they do not think they are worthy of having much of it, so instead of holding onto it and working with it to grow and to bring them more, they get rid of it as soon as it comes.

Meanwhile, those who truly deeply love themselves and know that they are worthy of lives filled with ease and abundance, use their Money as a magnet to draw more and more of it in ever increasing amounts, and they make wise financial decisions to insure their financial comfort and ease now and in the future.

Makes sense?

So, what does YOUR Money mirror say? How do you interact with the Money that comes your way?

THE "Make Me Good with Money" BOOK

Are you comfortable and making friends with Money, or uncomfortable and shoving it away from you every chance you get?

Are you treating it with respect, laying out the red carpet and treating it like a VIP guest, or are you treating it like a three-dollar whore, using it for cheap thrills and fading trinkets with no long-term commitment or benefit?

$$$

Activity 1.2

Reflect on your behaviors around Money and write it all down:

- Are you respecting it?

- Are you *leveraging* or using it as a tool to give you and those you care about a better life now *and* in the future?

- Do you understand that keeping and growing Money attracts and creates more Money, which means that the more you keep leveraging or use, the more you will have?

- Or are you like a starry eyed, inexperienced teenager spending every dime on things that have little future value and bring you no future financial returns and no peace of mind?

$$$

It's ok, no judgement. The more honest you can be about where you are at, the better your odds are of addressing those things and doing better in the future.

Money can be a wonderful friend, support and tool, if you understand how to best interact with it when it comes. Reverend Ike [look him up on YouTube] used to say that Money is a high-class lady. HOW should a man treat a high class, high maintenance lady? Well, start thinking of your relationship with Money the same way, and adjust yourself and your behavior accordingly.

"Listen to discipline and become wise, and never neglect it." ~ Proverbs 8 vs 33

Thoughts for meditation and affirmation

- *Money is an abundant and renewable resource, and I must respect and use it with reverence.*

- *Money takes various forms – e.g. solid (land, businesses and other hard assets), liquid (cash), gas (electronic assets like stocks and bonds) – and is always there surrounding us, in one form or another.*

- *Money should NEVER be prevented from flowing because stagnant Money brings decrease, debt, and disappointment.*

- *In order to have all the Money I need, I must collect it in the necessary amounts and sizes of containers. Therefore, I must first be abundantly clear on exactly **what** I require Money for, and I must have a detailed plan.*

Chapter 2

"I need help. Where do I begin?"

Glad you asked! You've come to the right place.

Now, as Riri said - get ready to werk, werk, werk, werk, werk!

"There is benefit in every kind of hard work". ~ Proverbs 14 vs 23

Are you committed to fixing your Money story? Ok then, let's get to work!

The first step is to create space.

Huh? Why space?

Well, because Money needs to flow. It requires space, just like a river. Money doesn't do well with clutter and obstacles in its way.

$$$

Activity 2.1

- Throw out old, broken things because no, you're NOT going to get around to having them fixed.

- Give away things that are in *good* condition – no stains, no holes, no rips, no missing parts – clean them up and take pride in the ability to pass on something that served you well, to someone else who will cherish it.

- Those clothes that you outgrew two sizes ago, give them away boo. When the gym and diet finally work, purchase new things.

- Empty your fridge and clean shelf by shelf. Discard all the almost empty bottles and packs of condiments too.

- Throw away the old school or work notes and books. It's ok, go ahead – no one will die.

- The old ceramics from Mommy that you're holding onto because they were gifts, give them to the next school that's looking for bran tub donations for their fair.

- Old makeup? Toss it.

- The collection of bottles under the kitchen and bathroom sinks? Yep, those too.

- The child's first teddy missing one eye and a leg, mmhmm, yep, tell teddy thanks and let teddy go.

Clear it all out.

$$$

Step two is *'Get to cleaning'*, just like Ma said.

Activity 2.2

Deep clean your home: EVERY surface – ledges, sides, undersides, places people cannot see ... ESPECIALLY places people cannot see.

- Move the furniture.
- Dust the corners.
- Cobweb everywhere.

- Sweep, mop and scrub.

Get a good workout and sweat – your body will thank you.

Remember, how you handle small things is how you will handle big things. The way you clean and the thoroughness you do it with or not, says A LOT about how your life is, your level of excellence and the peace of mind that you have or don't have.

The significance of this decluttering and cleaning is as much energetic and psychological as it is physical. You **deserve** to live in a decluttered, clean home. You **deserve** to be surrounded by functional, new, and beautiful things. Think of all the wealthy people's homes you have ever seen. What do they have in common? Let's list a few things:

- Lots of space – you could literally play small goal football in some of these places, and there's not much furniture to have to move either.

- Light and airy – lots of windows, mirrors and glass, tall ceilings, tons of lights and lamps.

- Beautiful things – art on the walls, sculptures, gorgeous rugs, lovely glass pieces, even the furniture is gorgeous.

- Water features – ever notice that there's always a pool, a fountain, a lake, something?? Because water and Money mimic each other energetically.

- Quality – you can tell just by the look and "feel" in a wealthy person's home, that you're surrounded by quality. When you buy quality, it lasts. Their homes don't have patched together or falling apart things, because they know they're worthy of better.

- Clean – hell, they even employ people to keep their homes and yards clean, because they know Ma was kinda right – cleanliness is next to financial success.

Always keep the list above in mind when thinking of keeping something broken rather than purchasing something new, and in terms of your habits of cleanliness. Ask yourself — What would the wealthy do?

Also, you want to always think of Money as a VIP guest. If the Obamas or some other famous couple that you admire were coming to visit a week from today, what changes would you make around your home between now and then? Do the same for Money. I promise you won't

regret it.

Thoughts for meditation and affirmation

- *The state of my home reflects my willingness to have abundance and good things in my life.*

- *The way I treat my home and the way I treat Money are one and the same.*

- *The state of my home attracts or repels my Money and abundance.*

- *Money needs a clean space to flow into and rest. I must treat it the way I would treat a VIP guest.*

THE "Make Me Good with Money" BOOK

Chapter 3

Ground Zero

Before we go any further, you need to take stock. It's time to look at the truth, YOUR truth. What's your current Money situation? Let's sit and create your **Personal Balance Sheet** to find out.

$$$

Activity 3.1

Get a blank sheet, recreate the document and fill in the following information as accurately as possible, to the last dollar:

Assets – valuable things I own that make me Money regularly and/or that I can sell for cash.

Estimated Value

1. (e.g. Paid off car in good condition)	$
2. (e.g. Genuine gold jewelry)	$
3. (e.g. Stocks/Shares)	$
4. (e.g. Antiques/Art)	$
5. (e.g. Paid off building or land)	$
6. (e.g. Rental property I own)	$
7. (e.g. Paid off vehicle on the road for hire daily)	$
Total Value of my Assets:	$

Cash

1. In wallet	$
2. In bank #1	$
3. In bank #2	$
4. Credit Union – deposit	$
5. Credit Union – shares	$
6. Mutual Fund #1 (including Pension funds)	$
7. Mutual Fund #2	$
8. Insurance Policy Cash Value	$
9. Under mattress/ On top fridge/ Hidden in home or vehicle	$
10. Rental property and/or hire car income	$
11. Loan or other investment interest (including stock/ share dividends)	$
My Total Cash Holdings:	$

Debts – Monies I owe to people and/or institutions.

Debts

1. (e.g. Hire Purchase balance on phone/furniture/ electronics/ appliances)	$
2. (e.g. Car Note – Total balance still outstanding)	$
3. (e.g. Loan)	$
4. (e.g. Loan)	$
5. (e.g. Credit Card balance)	$
6. (e.g. Consumer items on lay away)	$
7. (e.g. Unpaid bill[s])	$
8. (e.g. Mortgage – Total balance still outstanding)	$
Total Monies I Owe:	$

Totals

1. Total Assets	$
2. Total Liabilities	$
3. Total Net Worth	$

Do your assets and cash outweigh your debts? If yes, by how much? If it's by ten thousand dollars and more, CONGRATULATIONS!!! You're on the right track and doing beautifully!

If your assets and cash only outweigh your owing by less than ten thousand dollars, you're headed in the right direction but you're in the novice category, if your end goal is financial comfort and freedom.

However, if your assets and cash do NOT outweigh your owing, you my friend have urgent work to do! It doesn't matter whether it's by $5 or $50,000, you NEVER want to be in a position where you're in the red. Your being in that position tells us that you don't understand how Money works and what you're supposed to do with it. Not to worry though, the following chapters will help to steer you in the right direction, *if* you're committed to making the tough decisions, implementing the uncomfortable changes and doing the work.

Activity 3.2

Write down exactly what your financial position is, how you feel about it, and the actions you took to get there - good or not so good.

- Are you proud of yourself, or are you ashamed?

- Are you doing well or is there room for improvement?

- Are you ok to do this work on your own, or do you think you may be in over your head and need to find the right people to ask for help?

What about your decisions and behaviours?

- Did you act on impulse?
- Did you overextend yourself?
- Did you ignore the good advice of others?

- Did you take advice from those who didn't know what they were talking about aka they are also in debt or broke?

- Or perhaps you DID get the right advice and information and now you need more in order to move to the next level?

- What's next in your journey of doing better with your finances?

$$$

Thoughts for meditation and affirmation

- I must always owe less than I own, if I am to always be in a healthy financial position.

- I can change my poor Money habits at any time, by simply making a firm decision and taking new action consistently.

- Where I am today is not an indication of where I will be in three months, six months or next year. My Money outcome is up to me.

- I am excited about my financial future, because I will make the right decisions and take the correct actions to keep me in a good financial position, and even if I make a mistake, I will keep moving forward.

THE "Make Me Good with Money" BOOK

Chapter 4

"Wait, you're trying to say that there are people who have no debt? HOW??"

Well my dear, debt is a choice.

Yes, you read right – hire purchase, a credit card, a car note, a mortgage... all those are choices not necessities, and there are many people who understand that they're in a far better financial situation if they DON'T choose those things.

A common piece of wisdom among the wealthy when they're considering purchases costing hundreds and up, says **"If you can't afford to buy it cash then you can't afford it."** There's another saying that takes the idea even further - **"If you can't afford to buy it twice i.e. to buy two of it, then you shouldn't buy it at all."** Not sure I agree with the 2nd statement as I find it a bit extreme, but it still makes a valuable point about ensuring the strength of your financial position BEFORE you go spending Money, doesn't it?

Have you been living your life guided by *either* of these principles? If not, it's pretty simple to figure out why you're in debt.

When it comes to Money, *delayed gratification* is the game and '**Double your dollar BEFORE spending it**', is the golden rule.

Now, it's not your fault if the information above sounds like complete nonsense to you – it's how you've been conditioned from the day you were born; I get it.

We have always been told that in order to adult, we MUST have the (MANY) nice clothes, the credit card, the new shiny car and the mortgage. I'm saying, however, that just because you've been told something all your life does not mean that what you've been told is accurate. If that were the case, we'd all be well adjusted emotionally, in the best shape physically, successful in our careers, **and** wealthy. Or at least our parents and their friends would be, since we get most of our life advice and conditioning from them.

Think about it. If all the people who've been giving you advice all the years knew what they were saying, or if what they were saying was accurate, we'd be able to SEE the success, the ease, the daily peace, joy, and the contentment, wouldn't we? If we can't, then it must mean that the information they're working with is broken, but they continue to pass it along because it's all they know.

"A wise person listens and takes in more instruction; A man of understanding acquires skillful direction."

~ Proverbs 1 vs 5

A wealthy person once said, *"Money DOES buy happiness, but poor people wouldn't know that, because they've never had any"*. There are Bible verses that say **"Money answers all things"** [Ecclesiastes 10:19] and **"A good man leaves an inheritance to his children's children"** [Proverbs 13:22]. So even the Bible is delivering Money memos that many folks seem just to not have gotten.

Alright, so we're sure after looking around our lives that most people sharing "truths" about Money and what to do with it as an adult don't know what they're talking about. Now let's begin the work of reconditioning your thinking to set you on a path towards success with your finances.

$$$

Activity 4.1

If you had to take EACH payment or cheque you receive and double it BEFORE beginning to spend from it, as in LITERALLY you doubled EVERY dollar, what would or could you do? E.g. You start with $1500 and you MUST end up with $3000, or else NO spending.

Come on, be creative.

Write a list of no less than 25 ways. Yes, there are hundreds (yes hundreds) of ways

THE "Make Me Good with Money" BOOK

you could actually double your Money over the next few days to two weeks, so get to work.

$$$

After you have completed your list (and it must be realistic – so please don't tell me you could give music lessons if you cannot even play or read a note of music), figure out which 3 things you could actually do, starting tomorrow. Yes, tomorrow. You're in debt and need to get out, remember? It's simple, really. Figure out the logistics, who you'd need to talk to, what you'd need to get, do all that, and then start. It's time to werk chile!

Most people at this stage would begin with the easiest method – selling new, never used items or second-hand items in good condition that they have lying around the house, i.e. Thrifting. They would also look at the possibilities of a part time hustle – a few extra hours in the evening or on a weekend. Others would figure out how to earn Money from something that they do now anyway, like cooking, baking or cleaning. And some would look at how they could increase their responsibilities and/or their hours at work, in order to increase their take home pay.

Now is not the time for pride or for making excuses so you can continue to lie in bed watching Netflix… you have a financial problem to fix - that YOU got yourself into, so come on now!

Let's make it a game. How much extra easy Money do you think you could make tomorrow? Really, think about it. While driving to and from work could you pick up a commuter or two going in your direction and accept the taxi fare? Could you bake cookies or brownies tonight and sell them at work tomorrow, or send them with your child so they could sell them at school? Could you wash wifey's/hubby's or your parents' cars tomorrow and earn the Money they would have otherwise paid someone else? How can you easily finesse some more Money into your wallet tomorrow, legally and ethically, with not too much work?

See, when you really start thinking about it, the possibilities just start showing up! If you could earn yourself an extra $20 EASILY EVERY day, (we'll discuss what to do with it in a later chapter), why wouldn't you??

The reason most people stay broke, in debt and ultimately poor, is because they pass up TONS of opportunities EVERY single day, to get, earn and **keep** extra Money. Meanwhile, there are many of us out here in these streets happily finessing and *keeping* that Money, so we can meet our long-term financial goals!

Why don't you try it too? Don't you want to be financially comfortable for real (not just in image...and we'll talk about THAT later) or even wealthy? Because it's not as hard as you might think.

$$$

Activity 4.2

Speaking about wealthy folks, what do you "know" about them and how they deal with Money? Write down all the things in a nice list - as many as you can. We're going to discuss them in the next chapter and see if you REALLY understand the wealthy and how they interact with Money.

$$$

Thoughts for meditation and affirmation

- Debt is a choice. I can choose differently and create a better financial story for myself.

- If I can't afford to buy something cash then I can't afford it.

- I must always seek to double my dollars BEFORE I start to spend them.

Chapter 5

What do the wealthy do with Money?

Many, many people think that they know and understand how the wealthy live, because they think that the people they see in the media are wealthy. This misconception is responsible for possibly 90% of people being misled into debt and poor financial habits that keep them shackled and broke for the rest of their lives.

So, let's examine your list.

If you said things like the wealthy:

- shop whenever they feel like it;
- always swipe their credit cards to pay for things;
- take vacations all the time;
- live in huge houses with dozens of servants;

- own multiple expensive cars;

- wear only designer brands and tons of expensive jewelry;

- eat out every night at expensive places, enjoying lavish meals and lots of alcohol;

- pay people to do everything for them;

- use golden toilet paper;

- throw huge parties every week;

- send their children to exclusive private schools;

- own boats;

- have the most expensive EVERYTHING;

- spend any amount of Money they want, whenever they want, on anything they want; and so on, then …

Congratulations!!!

You DO NOT understand wealth or the wealthy.

Now that we've taken care of that, let me explain a few things to you and tell you the truth.

Wealth is measured by a benchmark called **Net Worth**.

If you're not sure what it is, Net Worth is the total we get when we do your Personal Balance Sheet (which is the exercise you did in Chapter 3). So we add the value and income from your assets, the cash you have in hand and in various accounts, monies owed to you and any guaranteed investment income, then we subtract ALL the Money you owe, from that total. Whatever is left, is your Net Worth. There are people with negative or minus Net Worth (because they are in debt) and then there are the wealthy, who have positive Net Worth in the millions and billions.

How do you think your Net Worth could increase?

Yes, by either adding asset value or asset income, cash, guaranteed investment income, or collecting Monies owed to you. Right. There's another way you can increase your Net Worth though – by decreasing your Monies owed, i.e. paying off your debts. And in the same way, you could decrease your Net Worth by decreasing your assets, cash and income, or by increasing your debts. Got it?

Now let's take a closer look at cash, for a minute. How would we decrease our cash in hand or our cash holdings in banks and other financial institutions? By spending it, right? Precisely. So *EVERY time you spend money, you decrease your own Net Worth*.

WOW.

The difference between the wealthy and the poor, broke and in debt folks, is that **the wealthy spend Money AFTER they have already MADE MONEY OFF THAT Money.** I'll say it again – the wealthy earn Money, use that Money to make MORE Money, and THEN they spend out of the **original** Money. Do you see how they win THREE ways by doing that?

1. They add to the Money they originally had.

2. They now have MORE Money to spend from.

3. Their Net Worth INCREASES EVERY TIME they make Money, and it STAYS increased.

And of course, with the new Money they made by growing the original amount they got, they rinse and repeat.

Now look at the way YOU use Money. Is your Net Worth increasing steadily EVERY TIME you get money in hand and also REMAINING increased even after you spend? No, right? And THAT is the main problem you need to fix. That's what makes you different from the wealthy folks.

I want to dig just a little deeper before we move on.

We just talked about cash and spending it, now let's take a quick look at debt.

As we saw back in Chapter 4, if you have a negative Net Worth i.e. more debt than cash, assets and guaranteed investment income, then it's usually because you act impulsively with your Money and you don't understand the Money game – *delayed gratification* – nor do you know the golden rule – **"Double your dollar BEFORE spending it."** I think it's also safe to say that you've either never heard, or you've been totally ignoring the wisdom **"If you can't afford to buy it cash then you can't afford it."** Now that you know more about how the wealthy operate with

Money, do you think they get themselves into debt? Hmmmm ...

Actually, yes, the wealthy DO use debt (note that I didn't say "get themselves into"), they **use or leverage** debt as a tool to grow their Net Worth. Is your mind blown yet?

Unlike in debt, broke, poor people who *get themselves into debt*, the wealthy USE or LEVERAGE debt specifically to ADD assets to their Net Worth.

Instead of purchasing a car just to drive around, they start a business and purchase the vehicle through the business, as an asset OF the business, adding value to the business Balance Sheet and allowing them to pass all maintenance and fuel costs through the business. Instead of purchasing a home to live in primarily, *the wealthy would get a mortgage on a property that has rental potential and/or accommodates their business*, so that they

USE THE PROPERTY TO EARN INCOME

which covers the mortgage and property maintenance. *The wealthy would take a loan to invest* in opportunities such as land development, purchase of shares/stocks that are expected to increase in value and/or pay **dividends** or profits, injection of Money to expand their business so they can earn even more Money, addition of a vehicle to their fleet so that they can reach more customers and/or be more efficient in their business (efficiency means more money), etc.

Are you beginning to clearly understand the bigger picture? **In order to have financial comfort, EVERY decision you make should ADD to your Net Worth either immediately or in the medium and long term.**

Now that you understand better how the wealthy carefully preserve and consistently grow their Net Worth, can you see that all the assumptions most broke, in debt and poor people make about the wealthy and how they use their Money, are totally wrong?

"Precious treasure and oil are found in the house of the wise, But the stupid man will squander what he has." ~ Proverbs 21 vs 20

$$$

Activity 5.1

Write a list of the things you know or have observed about the people who are actually wealthy. They generally have similar behaviours when it comes to their Money and lifestyles. Let me help you with some examples of actual wealthy people – Oprah, Bill Gates, Mark Zuckerberg, Jay Z, Warren Buffet, Wil Smith, Jack Ma, Lord Alan Sugar (UK) and Grant Cardone. You can also think of any you know of, who aren't on this list.

I'll also give you a few examples of [general] wealthy behaviour, and you'll see if you agree or not:

- They dress simple (no designer brands and outrageous outfits), unless they have a photo-shoot or red-carpet event to attend or dressing out loud gets them directly paid. If you didn't know who they were, you'd walk right past them based on how they dress day to day.

- They actually enjoy being at home and sharing home cooked meals with family and friends, and many drink no alcohol at all.

- They take the Money they earn and put it into investments like business equity, shares in companies, events that make good profit, real estate, jewelry and art that will appreciate in value, etc.

- They continuously buy into new investments, as regularly as the broke, in debt and poor people buy new 'stuff' that do not increase their Net Worth.

- They lease or rent spaces and vehicles for convenience and pleasure, for only the specific period of time they want to use them, instead of buying. They use their money or leverage debt to buy businesses and assets instead.

- If they DO own homes to live in, they generally purchase or construct modest homes, understanding that Money is better used to make more, instead of paying a huge mortgage and a huge home maintenance bill.

- They stay around fellow successful people from all industries, learning from them, sharing with them, dining and traveling with them, because they understand that iron sharpens iron. Kinda the same way that broke, in debt and poor people stay going out with each other to blow Money and have a good time.

- They always give to charity and they're careful in their words, actions and thoughts because they understand the principle "**What you sow, you will reap tenfold.**"

- One of their biggest investments is in the all-round education of their children – school, extra-curricular and vacation time activities, to increase their skills, life experiences and networks.

- Their day-to-day conversations revolve around their current investments, new investment opportunities and new opportunities for broadening their knowledge and experience via conferences, travel, meeting new successful people and being on the board of organisations in industries that they would like to explore more.

- As a rule, they purchase understated quality that will last for decades, never loud brands that everyone knows and that may actually be of a lower quality.

Of course there are always exceptions, but again, these are the general principles that the truly wealthy live by.

The confusion about who is wealthy and how they behave occurs because most broke, in debt and poor people spend hours of their time each week glued to the television and/or the internet, soaking up who the media tells them is rich, and what the media tells them rich people do. Except... the media is owned by a group of people who NEED you to go out and get loans and mortgages you can't afford and to keep swiping your credit cards for purchases of things that have no real benefit to your Net Worth, because THAT'S THEIR business - they create and maintain their wealth off of you by getting very well paid to advertise TO you.

See where you get caught in the loop? You're an asset for the people who market to you every hour. Your financial ignorance and the financial ignorance of billions like you all over the world, is keeping numerous industries afloat, at the expense of your financial wellbeing and your future.

"Do not be among those who drink too much wine, among those who gorge themselves on meat, for a drunkard and a glutton will come to poverty." ~ Proverbs 23 vs 20 + 21.

Thoughts for meditation and affirmation

- *The wealthy carefully preserve and consistently grow their Net Worth. If I am to be wealthy, I must do the same.*

- *In order to have financial comfort, EVERY decision I make must ADD to my Net Worth either immediately or in the medium and long term.*

- *I can learn to use debt to increase my Net Worth, instead of being used BY those who sell debt to me.*

THE "Make Me Good with Money" BOOK

Chapter 6

More About Debt

As you've realised, debt is (ONLY) a tool for increasing your Net Worth. Of course, as with any tool, it can be misused and cause devastating results, which it sadly is, all over the world.

There is a group of people who use debt to their financial advantage, but unlike many other wealthy people who hurt no one else when they use or leverage debt, this group of people leverages debt by hurting billions of ignorant people across the world. Do you know who they are?

These people belong to financial institutions, and they use the financial ignorance of the masses to their advantage, earning billions of dollars each quarter by selling more and more people into debt. Yes, **they sell you into debt**.

Look at all the marketing campaigns for credit cards, loans, mortgages, hire purchase plans, pay later plans, pay day loans, etc. Why do you think they would market these things to you so hard? *Because they earn millions every month from doing so; that's why.*

Let's go back to the wealthy – they have the financial knowledge to understand that **debt is a trap unless it is going to directly increase your Net Worth**. Unfortunately, however, the masses don't know this, so they happily engage, racking up more and more debt, thinking that this is normal behaviour. Sadly, it IS normal behaviour . . .. for the masses, i.e. the ones who stay broke, in debt and poor for the rest of their lives, thinking they're doing all the right things, yet never achieving freedom.

I mean let's face it, MOST people think **that a home mortgage is a GOOD thing, don't they?** A mortgage for a house you now have to maintain, while already paying out thousands of dollars each month to the lender, that you won't own for another minimum 15 years, and that keeps your Money so tied up that you really can't achieve much else. *Add insult to injury, you pay the mortgage lender a minimum of 50% in profit on the transaction, when you add up interest and fees. Is THAT a good deal for you, the borrower? Never.* **Not unless you copy the wealthy and put that house to work for** you, earning you rental or business income, which pays the mortgage and best-case scenario, also pays for the maintenance.

No, I don't want to hear about security and rent being wasted money either. No one says going to the movies is wasted money, yet that experience lasts only 2 hours. No one says a party is wasted Money, yet you actually SPEND additional Money on clothes or drinks **and** the experience is short lived and forgettable. No one says taking a trip is wasted money, yet a trip too, is fleeting and intangible. Your rent allows you the use of a TANGIBLE asset (a home) for 30 days. That's a GOOD use of your Money, while your mortgage goes towards putting Money into your pocket via your business or rental income.

Hey, you don't have to agree with the advice, or to like it. I'm just telling you the difference between the broke, in debt, poor masses and the wealthy. What you do with the information is all on you.

Should we even open the Credit Cards can of worms, where the broke, in debt, poor people spend Money they don't have and can't pay back, then pay only the minimum interest forever, because the interest keeps growing at alarming rates? No? We're NOT discussing that on the flip side wealthy people use their cards ONLY when they KNOW the Money is there or coming shortly (and increased) to repay? Ok, let's leave credit cards alone then, and move on.

I WILL, however, take a moment to discuss car notes. Most people don't seem to understand that **a showroom car is THE WORST use of money - bar none**, because THE MOMENT you turn the key in the ignition and drive off, the item you just purchased loses an automatic $70,000 to $100,000 in resale value...instantly, just like that, meaning that you can't even sell it for what you paid and break even. You LOSE from the BEGINNING!

The insanity doesn't end there, however. Most people who buy showroom vehicles use credit to do so and **just like a mortgage, between fees and interest they end up paying the lender a whole (minimum) 50% more than the tag price. So, in addition to losing tens to hundreds of thousands on resale value** immediately, they've ALSO paid at least 1 and a half times the ORIGINAL cost of the thing, which equals tens to hundreds of thousands of dollars into someone else's **pockets**! Listen, does ANY of that make sense if someone is trying to ADD to their net worth? And yet, people proudly do this DAILY! WHY do they do this? Because they've bought into **the myth that a new car is the best way to go – it's not –** and/or they're trying to prove to everyone else (usually other broke and in debt poor people) that they have money. See why I called it insanity?

So, what we all should really be doing is either purchasing the cheapest showroom cost AND maintenance cost vehicles possible, OR purchasing second-hand vehicles in great condition, or leasing - so that maintenance and upfront and lender costs aren't yours to pay!

Pride has no place in wealth creation; remember that. We're not going for image, we're going for substance.

"Do not be among those who shake hands in a pledge, who put up security for loans. If you have nothing to pay, your bed will be taken right out from under you." ~ **Proverbs 22 vs 26 + 27**

$$\$\$\$$

Activity 6.1

Shop around for mortgage rates for a 1.5-million-dollar home and see how much you would repay in total after 20 years, at various institutions.

Visit at least 2 banks, a credit union and Mortgage Finance Companies. Be thorough – your finances are NOT an area where you should be cutting corners and taking the easy way out. This information will prove invaluable to you and to others

close to you with whom you can share it.

$$$

Now that you've done the groundwork and investigating, how much more than the "property value" of $1.5 million would you end up paying after 20 years at each institution?

Is that a good deal if you're not earning any income from the property? And we haven't even added the maintenance and improvement costs yet.

$$$

Activity 6.2

From your investigations, you should be able to easily figure out what your estimated monthly payment would be, at each institution.

Take the lowest monthly payment and see what amount you would have in 5 years, if you invested and increased it by 10% **Compounded Interest**, each month.

So for instance, if your lowest mortgage payment out of all the institutions would be $4500 per month, 10% of $4500 would be $450. If we add 10% to $4500 in month 1, we will get $4950.

In month 2, we would add 10% of that new amount ($495) to the $4950 and get $5445. In month 3 we would add 10% of that new amount ($544.50) to the $5445 and get $5989.50, and so on. That's how compound interest works – you calculate and add interest, then calculate and add interest based on the NEW amount, and so on.

Very quickly, you can begin to **see how magical compounded interest is - IF it's working for YOU, and how devastating it can be if it's working AGAINST you** (like when you're walking around with unpaid Credit Card debt).

$$$

- What are your observations?

- What are your thoughts and feelings about this exercise?

- Are you seeing where it MAY be better to pay a set low rent, let your landlord maintain the house, and use the balance of the Money that WOULD have gone to your mortgage payment, to invest and earn interest that you continually reinvest and also use to purchase assets which will make you MORE Money?

- Are you clearly seeing why the statement **"The rich keep getting richer"** holds true? Because they have financial understanding that most people don't, and they use it to continually put distance between their Net Worth and the Net Worth of the people who just spend their lives paying off debt.

At the end of the day **Money is math** and the math either works out in your favour, or it doesn't. The wealthy are the people who chose to go against the status quo to put themselves in a far better financial position, because they did the math and they **always ensure that the math, not the feelings and certainly not social acceptance [from broke, in debt people], works out in their favour, EVERY TIME.**

Thoughts for meditation and affirmation

- *In order to have a solid financial future, I must be conscious about how I use my Money in the present.*

- *Compound Interest is life giving to my finances **if** I use it to my benefit, but it can be fatal to my finances if I allow it to be used against me.*

- *It is up to me to learn the truth of Money and how to use it, if I am to create financial freedom for*

THE "Make Me Good with Money" BOOK

myself and my loved ones.

Chapter 7

Containers

Like water, Money needs a specific place to go, or it will simply flow past you and go to people who DO have specific plans, places and figures, or it will run everywhere, become formless puddles and evaporate. If you wish to keep your Money close to you and get continuous use out of it on demand, you must assemble or create the necessary containers — just like we have dams and water tanks.

The first Money container we'll look at is the one most of us generally use, that's always with us — the wallet. Yes, it's a Money container, literally.

The exact rules apply for your wallet as your home, so let's examine your wallet.

$$$

Activity 7.1

- If your wallet or purse is grungy and torn, get a nice new one.

- A lucky Money colour like red, purple or gold would also be a great idea!

- If your existing wallet is in good shape, then declutter it - all the business cards, ATM slips, old receipts and lottery tickets, etc. must be cleared out. A wallet is not a filing cabinet.

The next thing to consider is how you actually keep the Money in your wallet:

- Is it going from ones to hundreds, each denomination with all the others like it?

- Are the bills all flattened out with no dog ears or other folds or creases?

- Are they all facing either up or down?

- All facing the same direction as well?

THE "Make Me Good with Money" BOOK

Get your wallet and the Money in it together! Remember, **how you treat your Money is how it will treat you**.

Also, feel free to spice it up – rosemary, cinnamon, bay leaf, spice bark, anise, cloves and ginger are all known in various cultures as abundance attracting, so why not drop some into your wallet? The worst that will happen is that it smells lovely.

$$$

Keep your nice-looking wallet clutter free and keep your Money in order. *Say it with me – How I treat my Money is how my Money will treat me.*

After your wallet, the next most used container is accounts in financial institutions. *This is where your planning must begin.* What do you need Money for – what short term goals e.g. living expenses, short term savings and contributions to investments; medium term goals e.g. travel within the next 18months and contributions towards larger investments; and long-term goals e.g. owning a home, do you have? Each one of these requires its own bank account - some savings, some chequing, some mutual fund, or even a credit union account – deposit or shares - depending on when you need to get the cash out and for what purpose.

$$$

Activity 7.2

Sit and create your Money plan. What amounts, their purpose and what container would be best suited to hold each of them while you fill the container to meet your goal. Also remember to put timeframes, because **a goal without a deadline is wishful thinking**.

Keep in mind that this is a chance to start afresh, if you've been treating Money like a teenager would – disrespecting it, getting rid of it as soon as it comes and not reverencing it like you would a VIP guest. Be mindful, spend time with this exercise, and **really be clear on what you want out of life**. The time to set things in motion to get it all, is NOW.

After you write down your Money plan, it's time to go about opening any new accounts you may need to open. Each goal requires a different account. You're in the process of ensuring that all the necessary infrastructure (pipelines and containers) is in place so that you can effectively tap into the flow of Money and collect the amounts you need to fund your day-to-day life AND your dreams.

You will hear Money gurus say that you shouldn't save Money, and even I advise that, because **sitting Money loses value fast**. However, even to invest or purchase assets, you first have to build up a sufficient amount of Money in your container to be able to leverage it, so that's what we're doing here. This is NOT Money that will be sitting around unused and therefore shrinking in value, for years.

As we focus on your Money containers, let's not forget the most commonly found container in people's homes – the piggy bank or change jar. Save those coins kids. Every hundred 1c coins gives you another dollar to add to your bigger containers! It is important, as the bible says, to show respect 'to even the least of these'.

On that note, quit, stop, DO NOT throw away or leave coins at cashiers. ONLY poor people do that, and that's exactly WHY the wealthy charge you prices that give them an extra 1 cent here and 5 cents there, because they KNOW you don't appreciate and respect money and that you'll happily walk away leaving the change for them to put back into their coffers. Lucky them, stupid you. Put some respect on your coins! They are Money too.

Now go around your home, collect ALL the coins (ladies, check EVERY purse), and get them to the bank to convert into dollars.

That's unused, unaccounted for Money that you just have lying around.

"Do not despise these small beginnings, for the Lord rejoices to see the work begin, . . ." ~ Zechariah 4 vs 10.

Thoughts for meditation and affirmation

- I show my Money respect by how I treat my wallet and how I treat the Money in my wallet.

- I am responsible and ambitious, and I have a well thought out Money plan.

- I show respect from the least to the largest, when it comes to my Money.

Chapter 8

Make a Decision.

You're now ready to do better with your Money and give yourself and your loved ones a better future, so you need to know what's next?

Well...

If there is one thing that the Universe responds to, it's a decision. God gave us free will and (with the exception of Jonah) has always respected and abided by people's decisions. Imagine that – the Creator of the Universe and all in it, the Great I AM, will abide by the decisions you make. WOW, now THAT's some awesome power! So, let's make some [good] decisions.

Look over each item of your Money Plan. What have you got on there?

A home?

Nice cars?

Trips to places far across the ocean?

University education for you and/or your children?

A business?

What?? What's there?

Now, **do you have realistic Money figures for achieving or having each of those things**? If you don't, now is the time. Go back and review. After you've come up with a plan that should require 2 million dollars at the very least, let's move on. You didn't realise how much Money your dreams REALLY required, did you? **Yes, "just being comfortable" in our modern world means you've got to be at least a millionaire… at least.**

"The good man leaves an inheritance to his children's children." ~ Proverbs 13 vs 22

THE "Make Me Good with Money" BOOK

$$$

Activity 8.1

For each one of the dreams/goals/visions you listed in your Money Plan, take a few moments to meditate on it. Take deep, slow, 4 count breaths, and really visualize yourself having/doing and enjoying the thing you wrote there. See yourself having the Money to afford it.

Now let the Universe know

"This... (house/car/European trip/charity work/etc.) is mine. I will have it. I have the Money to afford it and I am grateful for receiving it. Thank you."

Repeat the affirmation for EACH of your Money goals, no matter how small. You can do each one going down the list all at once, or you can do one goal each day, or one in the morning and one before bed at night – however you wish.

Just make sure to get silent, REALLY visualize yourself LOVING the experience of having/achieving the thing in your goal,

and then focus on being thankful.

How does doing this exercise make you feel? Do you feel silly or doubtful? If you do, you may not actually want that dream/goal as much as you think, so go ahead and edit your list to ONLY things that you want, deep down in your soul.

You should feel happy, euphoric even, like a child on Christmas Eve, SURE that you got what you really wanted. You should be FULL of expectation and also confidence that you ARE receiving the thing(s) you have DECIDED you want. Again, be very careful – if you don't really want anything in your Money Plan, NOW is the time to take it off. **Never ask the Universe for what you don't want; you may not be able to deal with the consequences of getting it.**

Along with the decision to HAVE the things on your Money Plan, you MUST ALSO come a decision to be your BEST around /with Money. Again, remember

THE "Make Me Good with Money" BOOK

that Money is your VIP guest, so be on your best behaviour if you want the best out of it.

$$$

Activity 8.2

For each one of the dreams/goals/visions you listed in your Money Plan, take a few moments to meditate on it. Take deep, slow, 4 count breaths, and really visualize yourself having/doing and enjoying the thing you wrote there. See yourself having the Money to afford it. Now let the Universe know "**I . . . (your name) . . . am worthy of receiving the Money to afford this . . . (house/car/European trip/charity** donation/etc.). I treat Money responsibly and with respect in EVERY situation. Money is my support and friend, and I demonstrate this good relationship in all my dealings with it. Thank you."

Repeat the affirmation for EACH of your Money goals, no matter how small. You can do each one going down the list all at once, or you can do one goal each day, or one in the morning and one before bed at night – however you wish. Just make sure to get silent, REALLY visualize yourself LOVING the experience of using Money to purchase the thing in your goal, and then being thankful.

$$$

Again, if the affirmations feel false to you, that's ok. Keep saying [and feeling] them regularly (daily is best, but every other day or weekly is ok too, if that's all you can take for now), until they no longer feel strange, fake or weird and you can say them with feeling, meaning, good emotion, belief and gratitude.

I told you from the beginning that this was going to be work.

Thoughts for meditation and affirmation

- *I AM worthy of receiving the Money to afford all my goals and dreams.*

- *I treat Money responsibly and with respect in EVERY situation.*

- *Money is my support and friend, and I demonstrate this good relationship in all my dealings with it.*

THE "Make Me Good with Money" BOOK

Chapter 9

But I have lots of debt – what do I do?

I'm happy you asked. Let's jump right into **the foundation of financial adulting and progress – your budget.**

Think of it, EVERY company, EVERY organisation, even governments have budgets and must present them for debate and approval by whomever is in charge. In your case you may not have a

Board of Directors or a Minister of Finance, but you DO have a Money Plan which needs funding, and so *THOSE goals are what you must be accountable to, with EVERY Money decision that you make.*

Remember, **whatever you do with your Money today, directly affects your Net Worth right now AND in the future.**

There are a few line items that MUST be in your budget. They are listed below:

Long term Savings – you MUST have an account that you don't touch. This Money is for the far-off future and would be best put into a compound interest account/fund that GUARANTEES your Principal AND Interest.

Living expenses – life necessities like rent, childcare, food, clothing, toiletries, utilities, health insurance, etc. A chequing account is good for these or use the

Envelope System – Developed by Dave Ramsey (google him).

Medium term goals – this Money can be in your Credit Union deposit or shares accounts (against which you can borrow while you still keep YOUR Money AND keep earning some interest on it). Credit Union loan interest rates are wonderfully reasonable, so always, ALWAYS go that route, if you can… but still always do the research at other institutions AND do the math first, because every so often a bank might offer a better overall deal, you never know).

Long term goals i.e. paying the future – this Money should also be in your Credit Union deposit or shares account, or if available, in a compound interest fund that guarantees your Principal and Interest.

Debt servicing i.e. paying for past bad decisions – car note, credit cards, consumer loans, mortgage, etc.

Growth i.e. **sure** investments – mortgage ONLY for rental/business property; purchase of goods to immediately sell for profit; purchase of tools to offer a consistent and regular service at a profit; life insurance (PLEASE ensure that there's Cash Value and/or a Saver built in); etc. Why do I consider Life Insurance to be

Growth? Well, if I can pay in a few thousands/tens of thousands over the years and my family walks away with multiple millions when I die, then I think the math works out in my favour. That's all.

Quality of Life i.e. experiences and fun - Cable, Wi-Fi, shopping and eating out fall here. Yes, those aren't life necessities, and you ALREADY have too many clothes, shoes and household "stuff". Do you want

THE "Make Me Good with Money" BOOK

to be financially healthy, or do you want to be undisciplined, idle and entertained?

Budget Percentage Breakdown (BEST CASE)

Long term Savings – 10%

Living expenses – no more than 30%

Debt servicing – no more than 20%

Growth – 15%

Medium + Long term goals – 15%

Quality of Life – 10%

$$$

Activity 9.1

Go ahead and do your budget now. Group the things you spend Money on each month, into their relevant categories.

When you've done that, convert the dollar totals into percentages of your total income for the month.

$$$

If you're looking at your budget and your Debt, Quality of Life and Living Expenses amounts are way above the recommended percentages, you have work to do. LOTS of work!

"But my income won't change and I can't NOT pay things so what do I do?"

Well first of all, **you CAN not pay things – cancel your Wi-Fi, cable and phone plans and stop buying food outside**. WHAT?? Well, you're obviously not financially responsible enough to have them, so yes, please cancel those until you can be more financially responsible. Remember, you have long term goals of financial freedom, so let's FOCUS.

Second of all, **your income most definitely CAN change!** We covered that in <u>Chapter 4</u>. It's time to REALLY adult and start adding to your income on a regular basis. Feel free to go back and read chapter 4 if you haven't already done so.

The most financially responsible (and secure) people, have high incomes and low expenses. They work tirelessly EACH month to see where and how they can save Money and how they can increase their income at the same time, by always adding new income streams.

$$$

Activity 9.2

We're going to review the <u>Chapter 4</u> content again. What can you do starting tomorrow (or next week latest) to increase your income by $20 to $50 a day? Once you can consistently do that for a month, then all of a sudden, you begin seeing other, better opportunities for increasing your income by even more!

Simultaneously, how can you cut back on your spending by $20 to $50 a day?

Whether it's on gas, public transport, food, phone minutes, Netflix/cable/home internet (yes, there's a daily cost that adds up to the monthly bill), finding a more affordable place to rent, what? How can you keep more and more Money in your pocket each month? Could you perhaps start a container vegetable garden? What CAN you do?

Also, how can you save and/or invest an extra $20 to $50 a day? What would that look like at the end of the year? What do you really NOT have to spend Money on, that you can cut out and add that Money into your investment account instead?

$$$

All of this IS possible, once you put yourself into the frame of mind of a financial winner, a Money Master, and take yourself out of the frame of mind of a broke, in debt, poor person. Now is the time. You CAN and you should. You owe it to yourself now, and yourself in the future.

****

Before we move on, allow me to insert a note on **Emergency Funds**.

If you've read or listened to any Financial Advisor in the past, you would have heard that you should have an emergency fund of at least 3 to 6 months of living expenses set aside for those unforeseen things like job loss. Some advisors will even say you should have an entire year – 12 months – of living Money set aside in an account that you don't touch.

I have personal challenges with this concept, because Money sitting around for no reason gives me anxiety – it is being eaten away by inflation, it is being taxed if it's in the bank or it is at risk of being lost to theft or disaster if it is kept in your home, and all those things add up to LOSS. We're NOT trying to lose Money up in here!! No, just NO! My advice would be that your Medium-Term savings act as that buffer.

Therefore, IF an unforeseen issue pops up that cannot be solved slowly over time by diverting income from your investments or your creativity and cutting back and it MUST be solved like tomorrow, then please by all means, bite the bullet, put off whatever dream or goal your Medium - Term account should have been funding, and do use that. Why? Because I can't see the sense in holding onto Money to go on a vacation if you're in an unforeseen bind today - that you're not sure when or how else, it will be resolved.

As soon as the crisis is over, your creativity and cutting back should go into overdrive, to replace that now lost Money. Yes, that's how a savvy Money Master operates. Let's get it!

Alternately, you can put aside $3500 to $5000 within a few months and use THAT as your emergency fund. This Money can be diverted - again from your Medium-

Term fund (but NEVER your Long-Term fund) - or you can cut back on expenses and put those savings towards your emergency fund, or you can divert one of your streams of extra income, until you reach your dollar goal. Once that is done, leave those funds alone unless you have an option for a quick (30 day or less) SURE turn around that will GROW it, e.g. giving a loan to someone that will earn you interest (ONLY to someone who WILL pay back in a timely manner), or something you will purchase to sell at a profit within days, e.g. a mobile phone or piece of equipment for someone who needs it right away.

Your final option could (but should really not) be debt. IF you have Money in your Credit Union shares account OR you have sufficient Cash Value on a life insurance policy in your name, you can take a small (NO MORE THAN $5000) loan against one of those, which you'll pay off in NO MORE than 6 months. **Discipline, good sense and using Time in your favour, are the keys to financial success**, so don't go messing yourself up by taking on a debt load that's too heavy and dragging it on for too long.

A crisis is NOT the time to try to be "smart". DO NOT borrow more than you need, thinking that you can use that Money to make more. No. Deal with your crisis, pay off your debt as quickly as possible, and move on. You've been warned.

****

A note on **Insurance**

Insurance is a strange thing that you ONLY need WHEN you need it, and at that point if you don't have it, it's too late. That said, I feel it makes sense to always err on the side of practicality and good sense.

If you're operating in a tight financial space where you are trying to pay off debt and get your income flowing in from different streams, then I would advise that you just focus on a cheap (no more than $300 per month) life insurance policy – *Term Insurance will give you the most coverage for the least money right now, and can be converted to Whole Life with a Saver, Investor or Cash Value later on when you're in a better financial position, with your debt paid off.*

It's easy to argue against it but, if you die, you want to **at least** leave a few hundred thousand for your family and/or child(ren), to handle any bills you've left behind (including burial), and to have some Money to buffer them as they seek to replace your contribution to the household.

Once your Money starts flowing better, please do review your insurance pay out and increase the amount and do this every few years. Your long term goal for Life Insurance is that you have the maximum coverage legally allowed – with more than one policy if able, and the highest possible amount in Cash Value/ Investor/Savings added on.

At the same time, you should ALWAYS have critical health coverage (which includes disability and/or long term care coverage), and the younger you take it out the easier and cheaper it will be, so get cracking! I advise that you get a blanket policy (covers all major illnesses) and add cancer coverage (because cancer seems to be the new HIV – you just never know who will get it). Believe that this Money comes in handy if God forbid you require major surgery or ongoing care in your 40s or older, the exact time of life when it's hell and hella expensive, to qualify for critical illness coverage.

Day to day health insurance could also prove beneficial if you have a family unit of 3 or more, and anyone is wearing glasses and/or requires major dental work.

Basically, develop a life-long relationship with your agent(s), do your research to see where you have the lowest fees, the kindest restrictions, and the highest pay outs, and don't be afraid to go to different companies for different areas of coverage.

Keep in mind as well that *no matter how nice your agent is, they are working for commission first, so you MUST do your own research, across companies, to find YOUR best fit.*

"By wisdom a house is built up, and by discernment it is made secure. By knowledge its rooms are filled with all sorts of precious and pleasant treasures."

~ Proverbs 24:3

Thoughts for meditation and affirmation

- My budget is the foundation of my financial progress and success. I use my budget to control my Money, so I can win financially in the future.

- I owe it to myself now, and myself in the future, to control my finances today and always.

- I must move myself into the frame of mind of a financial winner and a Money Master.

THE "Make Me Good with Money" BOOK

Chapter 10

Moving Forward

Of course, if you're carrying thousands, tens of thousands or hundreds of thousands of dollars of debt, your MAIN focus **after** putting money into your Never Touch Long Term savings account, is to pay down that debt. Basically, until your debt is wiped out, you should be paying ALL the Money you've saved weekly, and ALL the extra Money you're making, towards reducing your debt, **paying off the debt with the highest interest rates and/or Compounding Interest FIRST**. <u>The aim is to have a positive Net Worth, and the ONLY way to achieve that is by eliminating your debt as SOON as possible.</u>

Although I don't believe in debt, there ARE a few times when I suggest it. Apart from debt to fund a **sure** investment i.e. one that WILL make you back your Money AND turn over a healthy profit, I do believe in Debt Consolidation, if you're left at the end with ONLY ONE payment to make, with a low interest rate. So, are you in a position to secure a debt elimination loan from your Credit Union at a manageable rate of interest and a manageable loan payment each month? If you are, I'd suggest you go that route. Better to owe and pay ONE creditor and clear your name and accounts with the others.

Some people advise using your credit card to do this. DON'T!!!! DO NOT EVER use your Credit Card to pay out large sums of Money that you do not have in hand to repay. Remember, whatever Money you use off your card is due in 30 days from the day you spent it, then it collects a minimum of 20% compounded interest EACH month that the ENTIRE amount is not paid. That, my dear, is a life sentence of debt. Walk away! Run, even!

If you are unable to qualify for a loan to pay off the majority of your debts but you can get a smaller loan to clear a few high interest rate debts and reduce your number of creditors, I would advise that you do so, <u>ONCE the new payment doesn't cause you to exceed the total amount that you're currently paying out in debt servicing each month</u>.

Ever wondered why they call repaying debt "Debt Servicing"? Because you're providing a kind service to the bank or Lender - increasing their profits with every payment. God bless you, dear, dear soul.

"The rich one rules the poor, And the borrower is a slave to the lender". ~ Proverbs 22 vs 7

$$$

Activity 10.1

You should be able to get your total debt amount from your Balance Sheet in chapter 3. You should also know exactly how much Money you have in total, sitting in various financial institution accounts (including mutual funds). Use this information as well as your monthly income figure, to have fact finding conversations with your Credit Union and bank Loan reps; find out if you can qualify for a loan and if yes, what you CAN qualify for.

If they say you are unable to qualify for a loan, find out exactly why, and ask what you can do to address that. Those actions need to be taken into account in your monthly budgeting. You want to move yourself into a position where you can one day Leverage Debt to earn income via purchase of an asset. Best to begin that process now, even while you get your financial house in order.

$$$

I said it early in the chapter, but I'm going to say it again. During this phase of paying down debt, please...PLEASE DO NOT neglect your savings!!!

No matter WHAT is happening in your life, **your savings are your lifeline**. They cushion you; they give you a solid fallback position, they give you options. **DO NOT cut off your own options by depleting or by robbing your savings** during this time, or EVER. If you do NOTHING else when the month comes, you MUST save. Even if it's "just $150."

Commit to yourself. Commit to your future. Commit to be your own safety and protection in bad times. Commit to being a disciplined saver. Literally, one day your survival will depend on it.

Thoughts for meditation and affirmation

The actions I take in my financial life today, will determine the quality and standard of my life in the future.

No one is coming to save me if I keep making financial mistakes. I must save myself.

I commit to myself now and in the future, to do the very best job I can do, with my Money. I deserve it!

Chapter 11

An Alternative Financial Road

If you're young enough and not yet caught in the trap of spiraling debt (and Net Worth), this chapter is specifically for you.

Most people think that their finances should go like this – credit card, student loans, car note, one or two consumer loans e.g. for Travel, mortgage, then more consumer loans on top of that, with a new car note every 5 to 7 years. Stop and ask yourself – who does this REALLY benefit?

Is your Net Worth going to benefit, following the road described above? No.

So, I offer you an alternate road that Money savvy people across the world have used and do use successfully, generation after generation.

1. Save on student loans by attending technical school instead of doing a degree. In the currently

saturated global market, people with degrees are everywhere, and the good income that a degree once commanded hasn't been available for at least a decade. There aren't even enough jobs, far less jobs that pay well. Additionally, in some parts of the world the government actually pays you a daily stipend to attend technical school, because the world has a serious shortage of people skilled in the technical areas.

This means that when you're finished school you can command high incomes, based on the law of Supply and Demand. You will also have the opportunity to migrate, as governments around the world are offering relocation packages to foreign skilled labour, to address their internal shortages.

2. Save aggressively while living with your parents and work a side hustle while you're in school and even while you're done school and working a regular 8-hour Monday to Friday job. No excessive hanging out and partying, purchasing of worthless items, etc. You have a long-term goal to achieve!

The aim in this phase is to grow your savings (and Net Worth) as much as possible and as quickly as possible, so that you can make a savvy investment, then make even MORE.

3. Secure your first parcel of land – once you've saved a minimum of $50,000 see if you can find yourself a small parcel of land that's free and clear for purchase [all necessary documents – state, utilities, Regional Corporation etc. IN the seller's name ONLY and paid up to date] or for at

least 99-year leasehold from the state and acquire it through your Credit Union once all is well. You can build your home on this land eventually, but in the short and medium term it can be used for planting crops to reap and sell at a profit, and/or leased to someone to plant on, to use for [legal] storage, or to run a mechanic shop or other open-air business that doesn't require too much infrastructure.

Or, even better, see if you can get your parents'/ God parents' / favourite aunt's / grand parents' help (via guarantee or cash) to secure a mortgage for a modest RENTAL property i.e. a stand-alone house, a combination of apartments in one structure, a town house unit or a house and annex in one yard, that you can rent out WHILE still living at home, and save that Money as well.

Of course, all businesses and investments require maintenance, so be sure to put aside at least 20% of your earnings each month in a separate Maintenance account, so that leaks and other issues don't take your budget by surprise.

Yes, there is also always the option of selling for a profit, but there is old wisdom that says, **"You never sell land"**, and I believe in that. **An asset** should be leveraged to bring you ongoing income over the long term. **Selling an asset is a short-term mindset, and a short-term mindset can prove to be a hindrance to becoming financially free.** That said, there ARE people who "flip" land and houses as a wealth strategy. They purchase them for as low an amount as possible, fix them up, and sell for as high an amount as possible, bank the profits, rinse, repeat.

You have to know your market inside out and be extremely savvy in your construction/renovation phase however, in order for flipping to be a worthwhile wealth strategy for you.

4. So you've acquired your property and you're successfully leveraging it to earn you steady monthly income. At this point you have options. If you're

happy with how the investment is working out for you, you may decide to go again, with the same type of investment. Alternatively, you may decide to acquire a different asset, e.g. a vending machine in a high traffic spot, or a backhoe or truck to rent out by the day.

Whatever you decide, understand that you are now a serious investor and businessperson, and act the part.

Get yourself a lawyer to review all documents and to draw up proper lease contracts, get yourself an accountant to keep your books and to correctly file all taxes and other statutory requirements annually, and so on.

The wealthy NEVER run from their statutory requirements, because they understand that it would cost them way more in the long run, in

fines and levies, and that's wasted time and Money. They DO, however, **LEARN THE LAWS** so that they can LEGALLY pay as little as possible in taxes and other statutory requirements.

Others have found great success studying market trends and buying and selling popular consumer items in small amounts e.g. phones, clothes, makeup, etc., or as mentioned earlier, in doing agriculture for retail - whether planting crops and trees, or rearing animals; some are successful in trading on the stock and forex markets.

My only caution with these methods is that you do ALL the research and properly weigh the risks involved. **The aim is to GROW your Money, not stagnate or lose it.** EVERY investment involves risk – that's the exact nature of an investment - but some carry more risk than others, so **you have to know yourself, what your skills** are, what your patience levels are, how big your network is and how influential you are with those people, what your heart and mind can bear in terms of losses, and how much Money you could stand to lose and still recover quickly, BEFORE you get into them!

"Wealth quickly gained will dwindle. But the wealth of the one who gains it little by little will increase." ~ Proverbs 13 vs 11

Thoughts for meditation and affirmation

- It is ok for me to take a different path to those around me and I can succeed financially.

- The faster I save and the more I save, is the earlier in my life I can begin investing and put myself on the path to financial success.

- Short Term thinking has no place in long term success. I must become a *long-term thinker, to ensure my financial success.*

THE "Make Me Good with Money" BOOK

Chapter 12

Keep Learning

We have come to the end of our time together. I deeply hope that this book has left you changed – for the better. It is my fervent prayer that you are now empowered and taking strides towards your financial goals and ultimate Financial Freedom.

Please know that you are really only at the starting line; there is much, MUCH for you to learn and much growing for you still to do. So, what now? I suggest that you look into the following authors and read their books, to guide you from this point and keep you on the right track over the long term:

Suze Orman – known as the "personal finance guru."

Dave Ramsey – pioneer of the Envelope System

Barbara Stanny – money has a spiritual and emotional side to it, and Barbara is the woman to explore them with

Do keep in mind that all three of these authors is USA based and some of their specific examples and suggestions may not apply to you if you're outside of the US (and I'm not suggesting that you should take their specific investing advice either), but their Principles are sound, **and that's what you need at this point – good, solid, time tested Money Principles to live by**.

Additionally, I suggest that you read the following books - they are invaluable for anyone serious about building a solid financial foundation and WINNING financially in the future:

The Richest Man in Babylon – George S Clason

Rich Dad Poor Dad - Robert Kiyosaki

The Millionaire Booklet – Grant Cardone

Each of these gives you solid, specific tools as well as goals that you can set for yourself and work towards achieving. They're the blueprints for whatever Money goals you would have set for yourself. Read and re-read them often, highlight, underline, discuss with like-minded people, learn, try, fail, try again and WIN!

And of course, do come back to THIS book from time to time, to remind yourself of the basics, and to see how far you've come in your understanding of Money, AND in your personal Net Worth.

I wish you the best of luck.

Come join our conversations over on Facebook and Instagram @teamviplife we'd LOVE to include you, support you and hear of your setbacks and successes!

Peace, Blessings and Light,

KAramel

THE "Make Me Good with Money" BOOK

Women's Wisdom

I took the liberty of collecting Money wisdom from a few women who in my opinion have mastered the Money game, and who were happy to share their top 3 beliefs around Money with you. The wisdom from these generous ladies covers all bases in terms of financial success and freedom. Happy browsing.

R. Guevara, mid-30s. Home based business owner:

- Money is like a plant, a pet, or child – feed it, care for it, respect its nature. Leave it alone and it will not stay with you.

- Establish a Credit Rating early – get a bank/credit union account as a teenager, take a small loan and put it into your savings, or apply for a credit card, use it to pay one of your small monthly bills, and pay it off on time EVERY month.

- Save at least 10% of every cent that comes in, in an account that you cannot touch easily. Tell no one. Ladies, this is your insurance/emergency fund for life.

THE "Make Me Good with Money" BOOK

F Clarke, mid-50s. Home based business owner:

- Pennies add up, so be diligent in your spending and in your saving.

- Loans and Credit costs extra Money. Budget for a year and know EXACTLY what each bill / spend / debt will cost you ANNUALLY, and not monthly.

N. Williams, mid-60s. Family business owner:

- ALWAYS hold back some Money from your monthly budget. Budget so that you ALWAYS have a little left back to hold, until MORE Money comes in.

- Do not focus on glamour or a car when you do not own real estate. Real estate can be used as collateral against borrowing in the future, for a necessary loan e.g. medical expenses, business and investment.

- Pay off your ENTIRE credit card balance EVERY month, without fail. If not, the bank will own you for life. Likewise, pay your debts, if not all on time, at least pay some, regularly. Maintain your reputation and good name.

D. Claverie, late-50s. Retired corporate accountant:

- Money value today is not the value tomorrow. Make the most of it now by **not** spending on items that are fleeting. Instead, spend / invest on items where your Money REMAINS as wealth that grows and stays with you long term and continues to yield increases in your wealth.

- **NEVER spend more than you earn.**

Even if your income drops, spend less and STILL save some part of it.

These principles have seen me through good times and bad.

E. Ashton, mid-50s. Human Resource Consultant:

- ALWAYS have positive energy around your Money and in engaging with it.

- Enjoy using / spending your Money and not feeling guilty about it, but of course, be responsible and save.

THE "Make Me Good with Money" BOOK

A Rochford, late-40s. Business Owner:

- Make sure you have that emergency fund for life's unexpected moments, that way you do not have to touch those long-term investments. $2000 to $3000 is good.

- Go for the aggressive investments for your long-term investments; Stocks and real estate CAN work for you.

A. Ceoline, late-30s. Career Investor:

- Financial security is work and it is hard work.

- Youth is a gift. There is a loss of drive from your mid-30s onwards, so you better do the work before that, to ensure that when the slow down comes, you're already in a winning position.

- Find out about Stocks, Mutual Funds and other kinds of investments and

THE "Make Me Good with Money" BOOK

how you can use them to win financially.

Glossary of Financial Terms

Asset - An **asset** is a resource with economic value that an individual owns or controls, with the expectation that it will provide a future benefit.

Balance Sheet - a statement of the assets, liabilities, and capital of a person at a particular point in time, detailing their balance of income and expenditure.

Budget - an estimate of income and expenditure for a set period of time.

Creditor - a person or company to whom Money is owed.

Debt/ Owings - a sum of Money that is owed or due to an institution, or person.

Debt servicing – paying the amount of Money required in a given period to cover the interest expense AND principal of an existing loan.

Dividends - a sum of Money paid regularly (typically annually) by a company to its shareholders out of its profits (or reserves).

Insurance - an arrangement by which a company or the state undertakes to provide a guarantee of compensation for specified loss, damage, illness, or death in return for payment of a specified premium, over a specified period of time.

Term Insurance: a type of life insurance policy that provides coverage for ONLY an agreed period of time or a specified "term" of years. If the insured dies during the time period specified in the policy and the policy is active or 'in force' i.e. all premiums have been paid to that point, a death benefit will be paid. If they die after that term, there is no benefit to be paid.

Whole Life Insurance: a type of permanent life insurance, which covers the insured for the duration of their life, as long as all premiums are paid up to that point and the policy is active or 'in force'.

Interest - Money paid regularly at a particular rate, either for the use of Money lent, or for delaying the repayment of a debt.

Investment – Money put into financial schemes, shares, property, or a commercial venture with the expectation of achieving a profit.

Leverage – to use (something) to maximum advantage.

Liability - the state of being legally responsible for something which is likely to put one at a disadvantage.

Net Worth - the total value of all the financial assets owned by a person, minus the total value of all their liabilities.

Principal - a sum of Money lent or invested, on which interest is paid.

Profit - a financial gain, especially the difference between the amount earned and the amount spent in buying, operating, or producing something.

Rental property – a property from which the owner receives payment from the occupant(s) - known as tenants, in return for occupying or using the property.

Rental properties may be either residential or commercial.

Shares/Stocks - one of the equal parts into which a company's capital is divided, entitling the holder to a proportion of the profits.

Sure/Guaranteed investment - an investment that offers a guaranteed rate of return over a fixed period of time.

www.ingramcontent.com/pod-product-compliance
Lightning Source LLC
Chambersburg PA
CBHW050132170426
43197CB00011B/1803